NANTUCKET
STEPHEN
GALLERY
HUNECK
MASSACHUSETTS

STEPHEN HUNECK GALLERY
32 Centre Street • Nantucket, MA 02554
508-228-9977

MY DOG'S BRAIN

By Stephen Huneck

Stephen Huneck
1997

PENGUIN
STUDIO

PENGUIN STUDIO
Published by the Penguin Group
Penguin Putnam Inc., 375 Hudson Street,
New York, New York 10014 U. S. A.
Penguin Books Ltd., 27 Wrights Lane,
London W8 5TZ, England
Penguin Books Australia Ltd., Ringwood,
Victoria, Australia
Penguin Books Canada Ltd., 10 Alcorn Avenue,
Toronto, Ontario, Canada M4V 3B2
Penguin Books (N.Z.) Ltd., 182-190 Wairau Road,
Auckland 10, New Zealand

Penguin Books Ltd., Registered Offices,
Harmondsworth, Middlesex, England

First published in 1997 by Penguin Studio,
a member of Penguin Putnam Inc.

10 9 8 7 6 5 4 3 2 1

CIP data available
ISBN 0-670-87736-0
Printed in Japan

Designed by Stephen Huneck and Hans Teensma
Production design by Impress, Inc., Northampton, Massachusetts

Information about the original woodcut prints
reproduced in this book can be obtained through:
STEPHEN HUNECK GALLERY
49 Central Street
P.O. Box 59
Woodstock, Vermont 05091
e-mail: HUNECK@aol.com

Verve Editions, Burlington, Vermont

★

This book is dedicated to all the dogs

that have shared my life and helped me to learn how to love.

I would like to thank the following people: Michael Lamp whose tireless

help in hand-pulling these woodcuts was invaluable; Lara Phelps Ranby at the

Stephen Huneck Gallery, Woodstock, Vermont, for her intelligence and humor; Robin

and Jay Fuchs at the Stephen Huneck Gallery, Nantucket, for their enthusiasm and

dedication to the arts; Michael Fragnito and Christopher Sweet of Penguin Studio for their faith

in me; Hans Teensma for his insight, and Gary Chassman whose vision made this book possible. ★ I

would also like to thank all the wonderful people

who have collected my artwork over the years,

Acknowledgements

without whose support I could not live my dream. To name just a few: Bonnie Reid Martin, Robert

and Patricia Stemple, Senator and Mrs. Patrick Leahy, David and Vivian Campbell, Gus and Kathy

Aguirre, Michael and Susan Freedland, Pedro and Claudia Vieco, Jules and Effen Older, Beth Ide,

Florence Maurizi, George and Leslie Devol, Jan Stephenson, Charles Hinnant, Paul Leaman,

Debra Mimran, Dr. and Mrs. Schiele, Reverend and Mrs. Stecker, and especially Alexander

Acevedo. ★ Our deepest gratitude to Sally's former home, The Seeing Eye

Institute of Morristown, New Jersey for their unending love of dogs and

humanity. ★ To my wife Gwen, our life together is an incredible

adventure. Finally, a thank you to

Sally, my muse.

Introduction

The wood block prints in this book are a direct result of the miracles of life and love. They express the importance of embracing joy, love, and laughter each day of our lives. ★ In the autumn of 1994 I spoke with Gwen, my wife and partner of 25 years, about a series of wood block prints I had been thinking about making. The subject would be our black Labrador, Sally, my frequent sculpture model and constant companion in the studio. I had only done a couple of wood cuts long before and was anxious to explore this new medium. Before I was able to begin them, however, I had an accident. I fell down the stairs in my carving studio and was knocked unconscious. Gwen took me to the local hospital where I was treated for minor injuries and a couple of broken ribs. So began the most meaningful experience of my life. ★ I developed Adult Respiratory Distress Syndrome. The recovery rate for this mysterious illness is less than 50%. It comes on quickly and without warning. ARDS found me in my local hospital and took over my

life. In a coma, I was rushed by helicopter to a larger hospital. If I have lived through ARDS, Gwen has lived with it. She never left my side while I was in the hospital, often sleeping on the floor of my room so that she could stay near me. She moved my artwork into the room and played my favorite

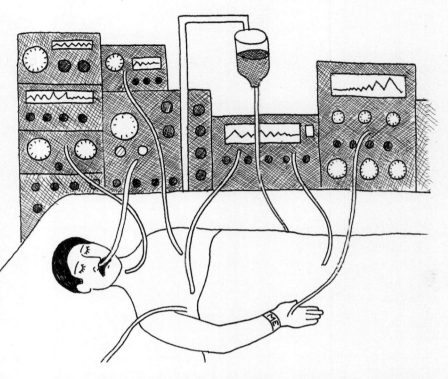

music. She spent her days talking to me and massaging my legs and arms. Doctors advised Gwen to prepare herself for the possibility of my death and were concerned when she refused to entertain any thoughts of the kind. One night they told her they didn't expect me to make it till morning. She stayed with me through the night, telling me she loved me again and again. In desperation she shouted, "You have to live, you have to do those wood cuts you were so excited about!" Together, we defied death. ★ When I awoke from the coma I could hear what Gwen and the doctors were saying to me but could not respond. I was on life support and the tube in my throat prevented me from speaking. Doctors told Gwen that I had most likely suffered brain damage. Given a pad of paper and pen, I wrote a message asking for wood and my carving chisels. I thought they should have been able to

read it but in reality my sentences came out as only "mmmmmm"s, further convincing the doctors that I had brain damage. Again, Gwen refused to accept their diagnoses. I remember so clearly the day they removed the tube from my throat. With three doctors hovering over my bed I croaked out a joke about the whole situation. I have never seen three people more shocked. One of the doctors gasped, "He's a comedian!" He later told me that at that moment he finally felt fulfilled as a doctor. For months he had dealt only with a failing body run by machines, not knowing the great spark of life that existed within me. ★ I believe Gwen's constant and reassuring words while I was in the coma had a very profound effect on me. They helped me to retain my optimism and sense of humor when I realized I would have to rebuild every muscle in my body before I could carve, or even walk, again. Transferred to a nursing home, I began physical therapy. My once massively strong arms were so weak that the act of turning a door knob would exhaust me. Anxious to leave, I pushed myself hard. Soon I was able to return home to my wife, my dogs and my studio. With trembling hands I began carving the series of wood block prints that evolved into this book, using the act of carving as my physical and spiritual rehabilitation. I remember vividly working on that first print. It is called "Life is a Ball," and it is.

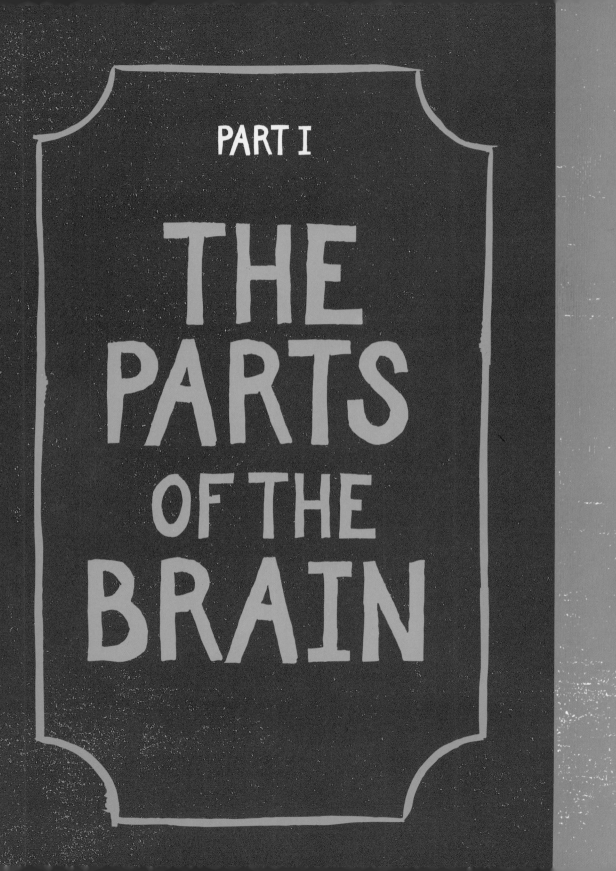

PART I

THE PARTS OF THE BRAIN

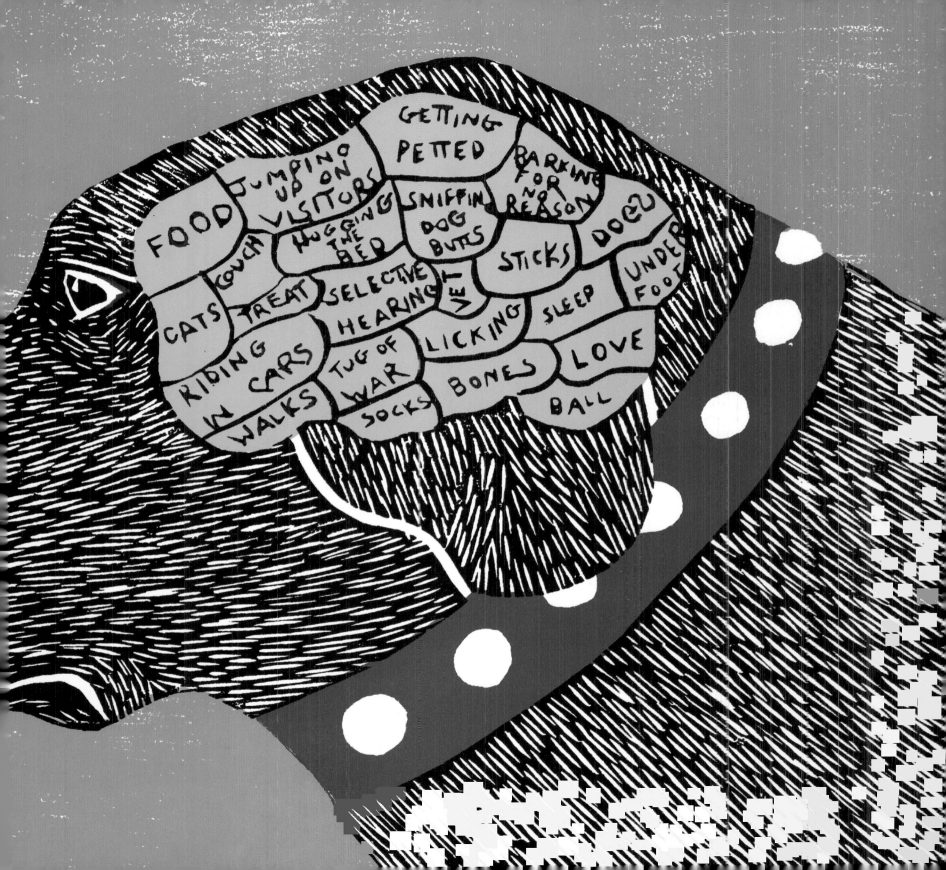

LIFE IS
A BALL

JOY
RIDE

GREETINGS

HOGGING THE BED

BARKING
FOR NO
REASON

LAP DOG

GETTING PETTED

UNDERFOOT

LIFE'S LITTLE PROBLEMS

SELECTIVE HEARING

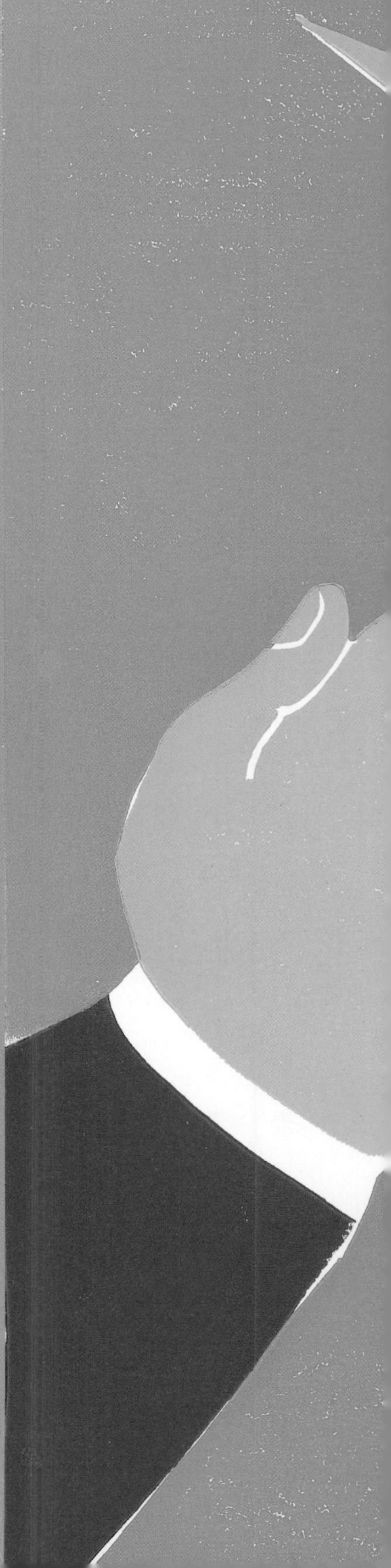

SOCIAL
SECURITY

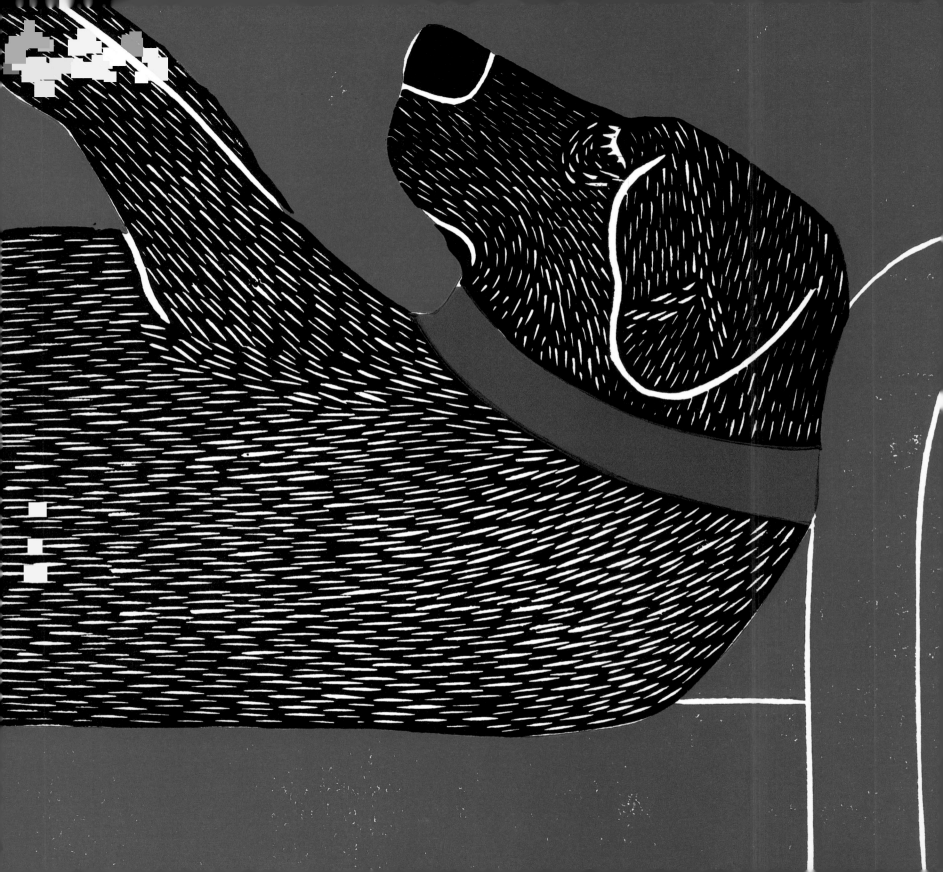

DOG BED

THE VET

STICKS

BONES

CATS?

GOOD SOX

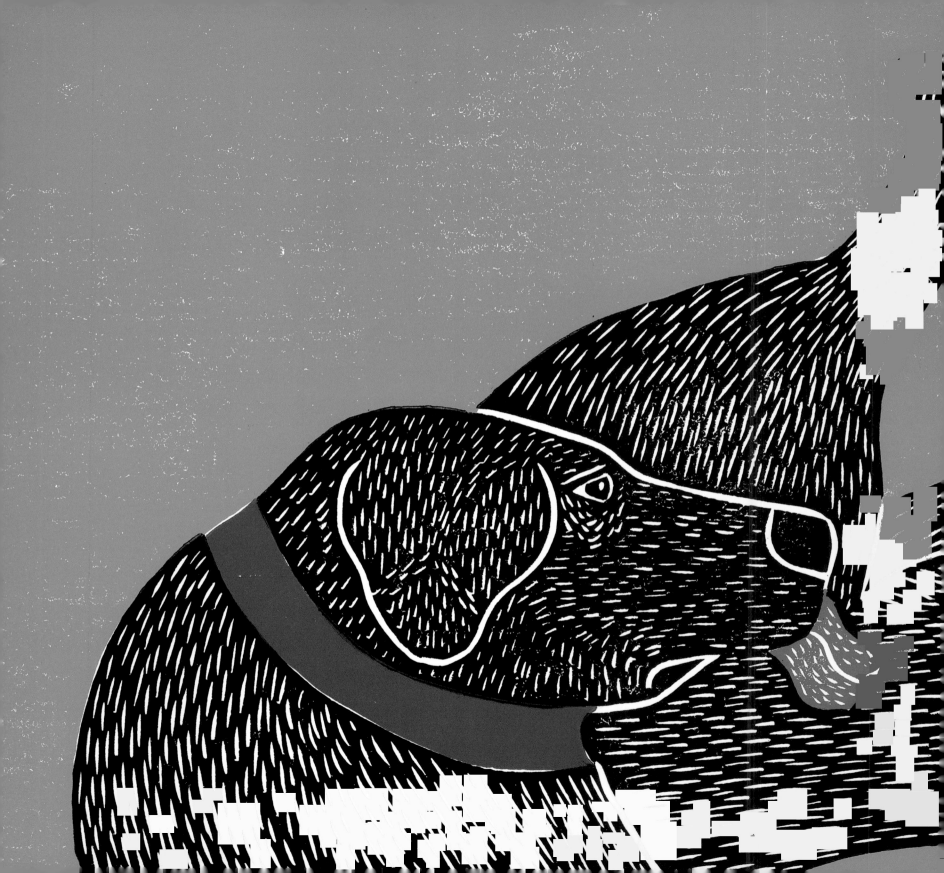

BECAUSE
THEY CAN

LOVE IS GIVE

AND TAKE

PART II

THE TWO HEMISPHERES OF THE BRAIN

GOOD DOG

NATURE

BAD DOG

WALK

GOOD DOG

GREETING

BAD DOG

VISITORS

GOOD DOG

FRISBIE

DOG

BAD DOG

TOYS

TO BE

OR NOT TO BE

WHEN IT COMES TO FOOD ANYTHING GOES

BAD DOG

GETTING A TREAT

BAD DOG

FAST FOOD

GOOD DOG

FETCHING

BAD DOG

THE PAPER

GOOD DOG

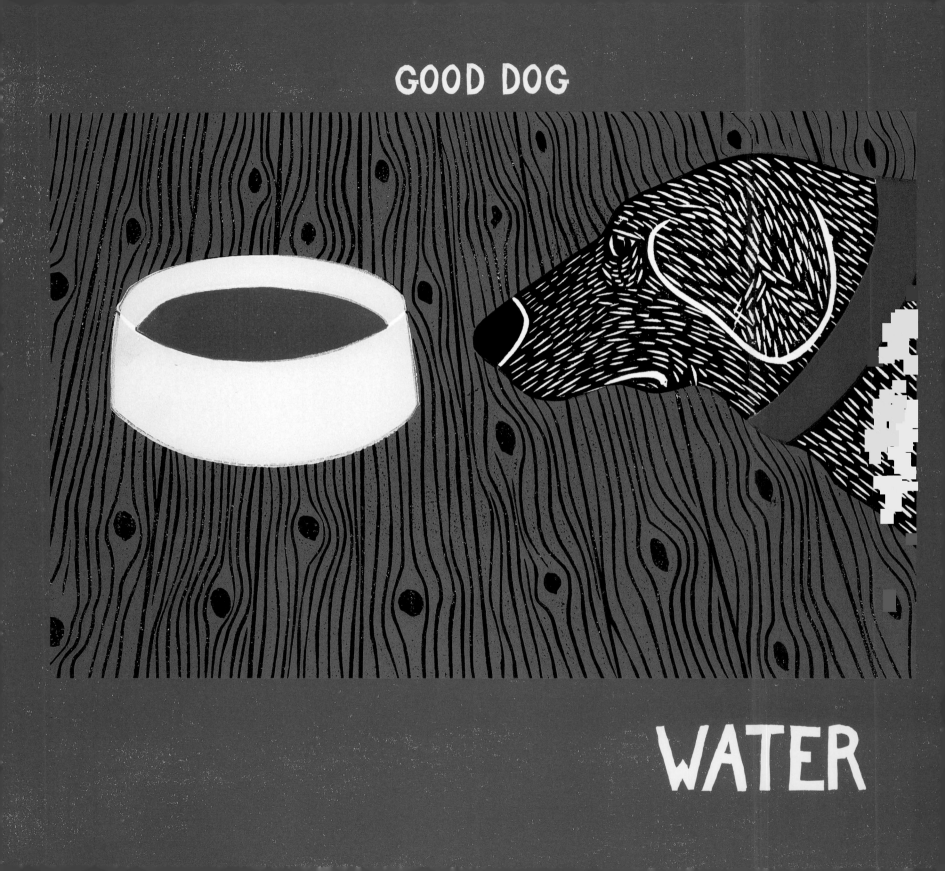

WATER

BAD DOG

BOWL

GOOD DOG

WE LOVE THEM

BAD DOG

JUST THE SAME

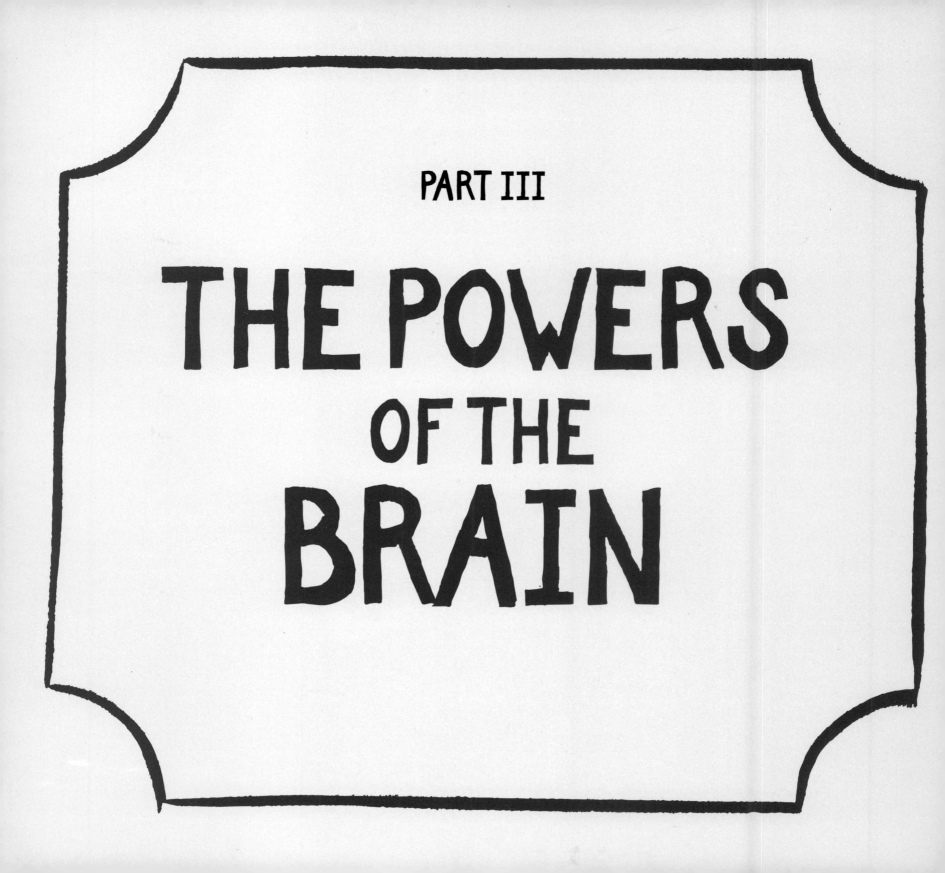

PART III

THE POWERS OF THE BRAIN

DOGS ARE
PSYCHIC

THEY KNOW WHEN YOU ARE ALMOST HOME

THEY SENSE
WHEN YOU ARE
GOING AWAY

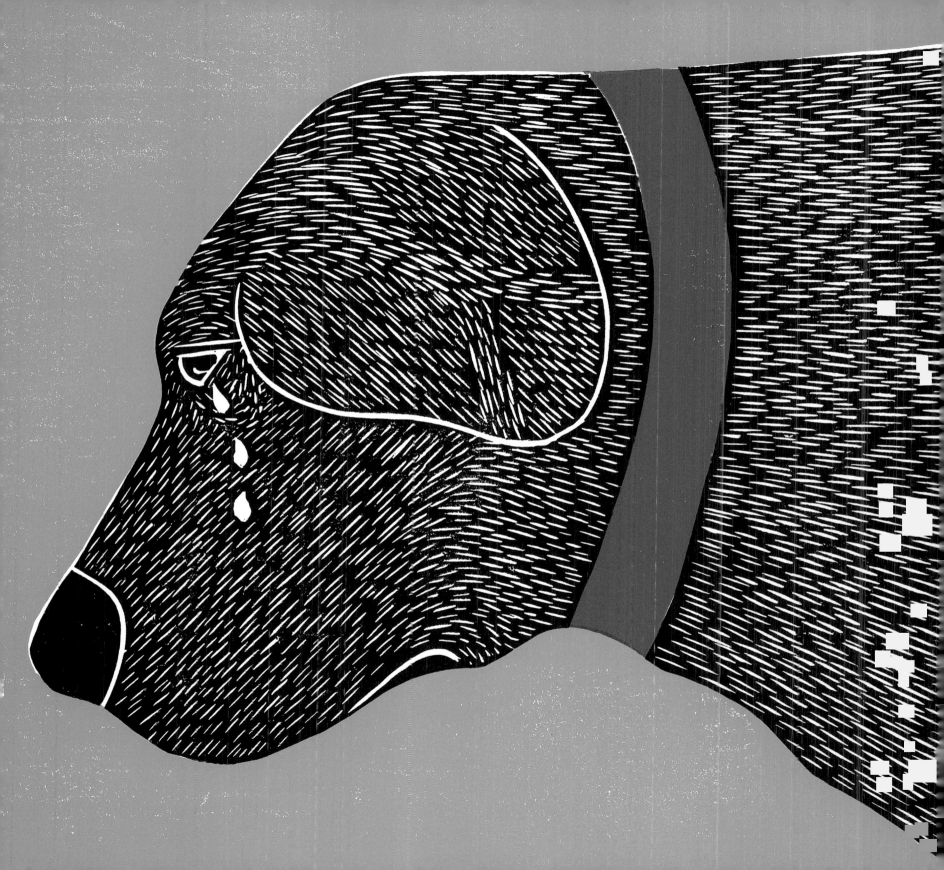

THEY KNOW WHEN YOU NEED LOVE

THE END